Surviving the Odds

Written by Claire Owen

Australia

My name is Ben. I live in the Australian city of Melbourne. Australia is home to many unusual animals. Read to find out which animals are at risk of becoming endangered. What is being done to help them?

Contents

Wherever you see me, you'll find activities to try and questions to answer.

A Changing Landscape

Australian Aborigines lived off the land for more than 40,000 years. They did not need to farm animals or grow crops. Europeans arrived in Australia just over 200 years ago. They cleared land for farming and brought in animals and plants from other countries. As a result, many Australian animals have completely died out, or become extinct. Some scientists believe that as many as 27 species of mammals, 23 species of birds, and four species of frogs are now extinct on mainland Australia.

The last known Tasmanian tiger died in an Australian zoo in 1936.

species a group of plants or animals of the same kind

Make a Pie Graph

To make a pie graph that shows the number of species that are extinct in Australia, you will need links or colored paper clips and a large sheet of paper.

1. Make a chain of 4 links to show the number of extinct frog species. Make chains of other colors to show the number of extinct mammal and bird species.

2. Link the 3 chains together to make a circle. Place it on a large sheet of paper.

3. Mark the center of the circle and draw lines to separate the 3 sectors.

4. Label the sectors and write a title for your pie graph.

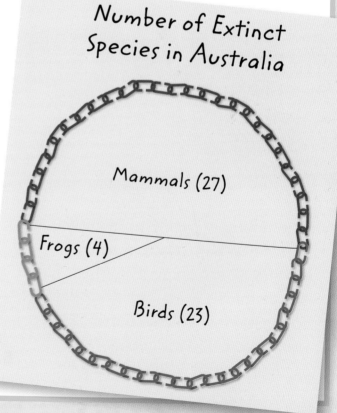

Number of Extinct Species in Australia

Mammals (27)

Frogs (4)

Birds (23)

sector part of a circle, shaped like a piece of pie

Under Threat

Today, many more Australian animals are under threat of extinction. A major reason for this is loss of habitat when land is cleared for houses or farms and forests are logged for lumber. Many native animals are killed by introduced predators, such as the cats and dogs that people from Europe brought with them. Other introduced animals, such as cattle and rabbits, eat the food needed by native animals.

The tiger quoll was once common throughout eastern Australia. It is now found in only a few small areas.

The mountain pygmy-possum was thought to be extinct. However, in 1966, skiers found one of these tiny mammals living in a ski lodge! Scientists now believe there are about 2,000 mountain pygmy-possums living in the wild.

habitat the place where something normally lives

Number of Australian Species on the Endangered List

KEY

Each whole symbol on the graph represents 2 species.

Look at the pictograph. What is the difference between the number of species of endangered birds and fish? What is the total number of endangered species?

Pictograph categories: Fish, Frogs, Reptiles, Birds, Mammals

endangered close to becoming one of the last left on Earth

Back from the Brink

The koala is one of the most popular Australian animals, yet this marsupial was once hunted for its fur. During the 1920s, more than one million koala skins were sold each year. The hunting of koalas was banned in 1927. Today, Australia has only about 100,000 koalas. People are now trying to save the koalas' habitat, and the good news is that koala numbers are rising!

Koalas eat about $2\frac{1}{2}$ pounds of gum leaves each day. The leaves provide very little energy, however, so koalas sleep for up to 20 hours a day!

marsupial a mammal that carries its babies in a pouch on its belly

THE
MAGIC PUDDING
Slice Three

Being still more adventures of
BUNYIP BLUEGUM.
BY NORMAN LINDSAY

Several Australian
children's books from the
1920s featured cute koala
characters. This helped
make koalas popular
around the world.

American President
Herbert Hoover banned
koala skins from being
brought into the United
States. This helped save
the koala from extinction.

Figure It Out

How would you solve
these problems? You may
use a calculator to help.

1. How many pounds of gum
    leaves would a koala eat—

    a. in 4 days?

    b. in a week?

    c. in the month
        of September?

2. For about how many hours
    is a koala awake—

    a. each day?

    b. each week?

    c. each year?
    (Hint: A year has 52 weeks.)

3. The first koalas in America
    went to the San Diego Zoo
    in 1925. They were a gift from
    the children of Australia. How
    many years ago was 1925?

Penguins on Parade

The world's smallest penguin is found only in Australia and New Zealand. The fairy penguin (or little penguin) spends four-fifths of its time at sea. Its feathers keep it warm and waterproof. Fairy penguins are the sea birds most likely to come into contact with oil spills at sea.

In the evening, groups of fairy penguins scurry up the beach to their burrows. This nightly "penguin parade" is a popular tourist attraction.

At wildlife centers, oil-covered penguins are dressed in knitted woolen sweaters! This stops the penguins from swallowing oil when they try to preen their feathers.

In 2001, the Tasmanian Conservation Trust asked volunteers to knit sweaters for penguins. The Trust received more than 15,000 sweaters from all around the world!

preen to make feathers clean and tidy

Saving the Bilby

A bilby is a small marsupial with rabbitlike ears. There are only two species of bilby. The lesser bilby appears to be extinct, and the greater bilby is endangered. Much of the bilby's habitat has been destroyed by cattle and rabbits. In addition, a bilby makes a tasty snack for a fox, dingo, or wildcat.

dingo a wild Australian dog

Peter McRae (right and page 12) is one of two Australians nicknamed "the Bilby Brothers." The pair raised $750,000 to create a safe home for bilbies. They built a special fence 16 miles long at Currawinya National Park in Queensland. The bilbies are kept safe in the fenced-in area.

Australians are encouraged to buy chocolate bilbies rather than chocolate rabbits! For each large bilby sold, 50 cents is donated to the Save the Bilby Fund. For a small bilby, the donation is 30 cents.

Suppose that 4,000 large chocolate bilbies and 7,000 small chocolate bilbies were sold in one month. How much money would the Save the Bilby Fund receive?

Raising an Orphan

Many people work hard to help save Australia's special animals. Zoos and wildlife centers play an important part in animal conservation. Young orphaned kangaroos and wallabies, called *joeys*, are sometimes raised by people. Cow's milk is not suitable for marsupials, so they are fed a special milk formula.

Did You Know?

Kangaroos and wallabies belong to a group of animals known as *macropods*. The word *macropod* means "big foot." Australia has about 45 species of macropods.

Figure It Out

How would you solve these problems? You may use a calculator to help.

1. About how much does a gray kangaroo weigh when it is 6 months old?

2. About how many months old is a gray kangaroo when it weighs 199 ounces?

3. Work in a group to make a new chart for the gray kangaroo.

    a.   Show age to the nearest week.

    b.   Show tail length in feet and inches.

    c.   Show weight in pounds and ounces.

A mother kangaroo or wallaby carries her joey in a pouch. At wildlife centers, orphaned joeys get to "hang around" in a cloth pouch.

Gray Kangaroo Growth Chart

Age (Days)	Tail Length (Inches)	Weight (Ounces)
120	5	19
180	10	43
220	12	66
250	15	83
310	21	199

Sample Answers

Find out more about an endangered Australian animal. Where does it live? What threats does it face? What is being done to protect it?

Page 7   22; 118

Page 9
1. a. 10 pounds
   b. $17\frac{1}{2}$ pounds
   c. 75 pounds

2. a. 4 hours   b. 28 hours
   c. 1,456 hours

Page 13 $4,100

Page 15
1. 43 ounces

2. 10 months

3.

Age	Tail	Weight
17 wks	5 in.	1 lb, 3 oz
26 wks	10 in.	2 lb, 11 oz
31 wks	1 ft	4 lb, 2 oz
36 wks	1 ft, 3 in.	5 lb, 3 oz
44 wks	1 ft, 9 in.	12 lb, 7 oz

Index